DANCE POSTERS

by Eleanor Rachel Luger

Designed by Jon Goodchild/Leaves of Grass Productions

A Fireside Book
Published by Simon and Schuster
New York

TO M AND P

A Fireside Book

Published by Simon and Schuster
A Division of Gulf & Western Corporation
Simon & Schuster Building
Rockefeller Center
1230 Avenue of the Americas
New York, New York 10020

Library of Congress Cataloging in Publication Data:

Luger, Eleanor Rachel
    Dance posters

    1. Dancing—Posters. I. Leaves of Grass Productions.
GV1595.D34   769'.4'97933   79-11823

ISBN 0-671-24790-5

Designed by Jon Goodchild
Manufactured in the United States of America

1 2 3 4 5 6 7 8 9 10

Title page: Niki de Saint-Phalle's joyous design for *Théâtre de France* for the Merce Cunningham Dance Company and Paul Taylor Dance Company.

Cover   Created by Peter Rogers Associates for Danskin. Photo: Richard Davis.
Title page   Used by permission of Gimpel and Weitzenhoffer Gallery, New York.
2, *Copyright page*   Cartoon, used by permission of Jules Feiffer © R76 Jules Feiffer, *This World,* Sunday, June 27, 1976.
5   Used by permission of New York City Ballet and Donn Matus. Design by Donn Matus.
7, *Right*   Used by permission of New York Shakespeare Festival. © New York Shakespeare Festival 1979. Photo montage: Paul Elson and Martha Swope.
8, *Right*   Used by permission of the Martha Graham Dance Company and the Metropolitan Opera, 1978. © 1978 Metropolitan Opera.
9, *Right*   Used by permission of the Martha Graham Dance Company and the Dance Collection, The New York Public Library at Lincoln Center; Astor, Lenox and Tilden Foundations. © Estate of Ben Shahn, 19—. Courtesy Kennedy Galleries.
10   Textual adaptation from "Toeshoes," originally published in the *Washington Post,* November 6, 1977, by Barry Laine. Used by permission of the author.
10, *Left*   By arrangement with the New York City Ballet.
11, *Right*   Used by permission of Stefan Czernecki, poster designer, Royal Winnipeg Ballet, New York spring season, 1978.
13   Used by permission of Los Indianos Guacho Ballet and designer Hector Católica, 1977.

Continued on page 72

Martha Graham Dance Company
Royal Winnipeg Ballet
Los Indianos
American Ballet Theatre
The Murray Louis Dance Company
James Cunningham and the Acme Co.
Capezio Ballet Makers
Ballet Hispanico
The José Limón Dance Company
The New York City Ballet
The Alvin Ailey American Dance Theater
The San Francisco Ballet Company
The Nutcracker
The Pennsylvania Ballet
Dancemagazine
The Houston Ballet
Nancy Meehan Dance Company
The Feld Ballet
The Luis Rivera Spanish Dance Company
The Joffrey Ballet
Bella Lewitzky Dance Company
Elaine Summers' Experimental Intermedia Foundation
Merce Cunningham Dance Company
The Lar Lubovitch Dance Company
Dancers
Dan Wagoner and Dancers
The Nikolais Dance Theatre
Andrew deGroat and Dancers
Met "Summerdance" Series
Dance Theatre of Harlem
Danskin

Introduction

Posters are among the oldest and most popular modes of communication, one that has been handed down to us through the centuries and that remains primary in our contemporary lives — even though they have long been surpassed in speed by the swifter medium of outer-space, satellite-relayed television. Posters, preceded in the very early days by the town crier, have evolved from printed handbills, elaborately painted hanging scrolls and placards into an important graphic art form — a time-proved, effective means of making advertising messages public. (The success of an event is often easily measured by the response or reaction to the poster that advertises it.) Almost as significant, perhaps, though not the *raison d'être*, posters are prime collector's items for those who cherish a reflection of some particular or individual passion — such as the cinema, the theater or dance. They recall the moment.

Dance posters are certainly among the most beautiful. Spanning the wide diversity of dance forms, they call into view the humor, grace and elegance of the art. They reveal its beauty. In time, they even reflect the mode of a particular decade or era.

The art of designing posters obviously advances with the age. Quality is judged by the standard of the moment. All the elements of image, color and design, photography, drawing and typeface are dependent on the skill of the creator. But the most successful posters are those which capture for a lifetime that very special essence of dance: the magic of a moment.

William Como
Editor-in-Chief, *Dancemagazine*
New York, 1979

Right: Donn Matus makes inventive use of contrasting background and foreground on this 1974 poster puzzle for the New York City Ballet. For those in the know, the words are ballet terminology — spelling out the names of ballet positions!

Preface

Dance posters are more than just pretty pictures: they entice; they inform. Graphically, through color and design, posters show how a company sees itself, while at the same time they try to make you want to come to see the company. Integrated into the visuals must be the event-related facts —time, place, date; perhaps ticket price and repertory. College campuses, and cities like San Francisco and New York with large "walking" populations and sections where artists congregate, such as SoHo or the Lincoln Center area, provide stretches of postered walls, rich "concert-shopping" ground for the dance enthusiast.

Drawing boundaries for a book concerned with such a broad topic as dance posters was difficult. I decided to gather as many posters from all over the United States as possible, and to represent as many different dance and graphic styles as possible. With few exceptions, the posters in this book have been designed in the last ten years and represent many of the major and emerging American dance companies: ballet, modern and experimental alike. In some cases I have included posters of foreign companies appearing in American houses, such as Los Indianos (Argentina), the Performing Arts Company of the People's Republic of China and the Royal Winnipeg Ballet, when I felt they were irresistible. Since the posters speak for themselves, I felt the text should speak for the companies, and thus I have written general company histories to accompany the graphics.

Many persons and organizations provided invaluable assistance for this project, and thanks to all of them. I want to specially thank Volunteer Lawyers for the Arts for putting me in touch with attorney Michael J. Remer, who gave me many hours of his time, and much encouragement; my editor at Simon and Schuster, Linda Sunshine; Henry Wisneski of the Performing Arts Library; typist Jo Ann Baldinger; photographer Karl Bruning and last but by no means least, Mr. B. Laine.

Eleanor Rachel Luger
Brooklyn, New York, 1979

Right: This poster for the hit musical, *A Chorus Line*, shows the dancers who make up the chorus line—and whose lives the show portrays. *A Chorus Line* was conceived, choreographed and directed by Michael Bennett and produced by Joseph Papp. Since it opened at the New York Shakespeare Festival Public Theater on May 21, 1975, it has been awarded the New York Drama Critics Award for Best Musical, 1975; the Tony Award for Best Musical, 1976; and the Pulitzer Prize for Drama, 1976.

Martha Graham Dance Company

Martha Graham is considered one of the leading dance figures of this century. She is known the world over not only for her gripping and revolutionary choreography and dynamic performance ability, but also for the movement technique that she developed and her talent to fuse all aspects of production — sets, costumes and properties. The Composers' Alliance acknowledged Ms. Graham's association with contemporary music by conferring on her its prestigious Laurel Leaf award; and her contribution to all the arts was attested to when she received the Aspen Award in Humanities. In October 1976, Martha Graham became the first dancer/choreographer to receive the Medal of Freedom, presented by then President Gerald R. Ford. The inscription on the medal concluded by designating Ms. Graham "a brilliant star and a national treasure."

The daughter of a physician, Martha Graham was born near Pittsburgh, Pennsylvania. The Graham family moved to Santa Barbara, California, when Martha was still a child, and she was enrolled in private schools. She did not begin dancing, however, until after her father's death, when he could no longer object to her interest in dance. In 1916 she went to study at the Denishawn School, and three years later she was performing solos with Denishawn. She remained as a leading dancer with Denishawn until 1923, when she left and found employment for two seasons with the Greenwich Village Follies. In 1925 she went to Rochester, New York, to teach at the just-opened School of Dance and Dramatic Art of the Eastman School of Music and to prepare for her 1926 debut solo concert. That same year she relocated to New York City, where Louis Horst began to serve as her accompanist and musical director, stimulating her interest in contemporary music and ritual dance. In the space of only three or four years, Martha Graham was well on the way to developing her own movement vocabulary and sophisticated solo and group dances. In the '30s and '40s, in addition to teaching at her studio and coast-to-coast touring with her company, she was active in theater, working with Katharine Cornell, among others.

The list of now well-known dancers who came to study with Martha Graham is lengthy, including Sophie Maslow, Anna Sokolow, May O'Donnell, Merce Cunningham, Erick Hawkins and Pearl Lang. Actors and actresses who have attended her famous classes in "movement for actors" include Gregory Peck, Kirk Douglas, Joanne Woodward, Bette Davis and Tony Randall.

Letter to the World (1940), *Appalachian Spring* (1941), *Cave of the Heart* (1946), *Night Journey* (1947) and *Clytemnestra* (1958) are familiar titles to dancegoers the world over and represent some of Ms. Graham's most compelling works.

Ms. Graham and her company made their first European tour in 1950; their second, in 1954. In subsequent years, the company visited the Far East — stopping in Japan, the Philippines, Burma, Thailand, Java, India, Iran and Iraq. On numerous occasions the company has visited Israel. The Martha Graham Dance Company also tours extensively in the United States.

And her legend dances on.

Martha Graham is bringing her company to The Met for eight historic performances.

From June 26 through July 1. Metropolitan Opera House

Right: Artist Ben Shahn created this lively poster for the Martha Graham Dance Company.

Left: Dark shadows define the long, slender neck and sculpted face of Martha Graham on this poster for the 1978 Metropolitan Opera House "Summerdance" series.

PHOTOGRAPHS OF MARTHA GRAHAM + DANCE COMPANY   USIS GALLERY   AMERICAN EMBASSY, GROSVENOR SQUARE,
LONDON, W.1.   JULY 25   SEPTEMBER 13   DAILY 9-6, CLOSED SATURDAYS AND SUNDAYS   ADMISSION FREE.

Martha Graham and Dance Company will appear at the Edinburgh Festival August 26-31.

Royal Winnipeg Ballet

What is the first thing every future ballerina learns — and the first thing every future ballerina wants? The five basic positions and pink satin toe shoes. Cartoonist Edward Gorey joined the humorous with the serious in his 1972 poster for the New York City Ballet (see page 27) with an exact representation of a pair of well-clad, perfectly positioned feet. The Royal Winnipeg Ballet elaborated on this theme in announcing its spring 1978 New York season. A pair of oversized toe shoes, poised gently on an open tulip, descend from a sky full of billowing clouds.

Though it is unknown exactly when the pointe shoe was developed, it was probably around the 1790s. An 1821 lithograph of the famous Fanny Bias of the Paris Opera offers the first pictorial record of a ballerina on pointe, but it was not until the great Romantic ballerina Marie Taglione premiered *La Sylphide* in 1832 that pointe work came into vogue.

The first pointe shoes were makeshift, stiffened with glue or starch and reinforced with ribbons or darning. It was not until later in the 19th century that the "modern" toe shoe was designed. This was a "box," a reinforcement of extra material and paste that provides support for standing on the toe. Contrary to popular belief, there is no wood, metal, plastic—or concrete—in a toe shoe. Material is pleated behind the toes, the sides of the shoe are reinforced and the bottom is flattened to provide a base for the toes. The box is merely a thick, stiffened end of the shoe.

Toe shoes are almost completely handmade, machines being used only to precut the leather and material and do some minimal stitching. The average pointe shoe weighs about five ounces. Only cotton/satin and cotton are used for the cloth materials; the shoe must both breathe and absorb. The shoes are numbered in sizes that run two to three sizes smaller than those of street shoes.

The Royal Winnipeg Ballet, Canada's oldest ballet company, evolved from the school and Ballet Club established in Winnipeg in 1938 by Gweneth Lloyd and Betty Farrally. In 1948 the company hosted the first Canadian Ballet Festival, thus giving rise to the Regional Ballet Festival movement, which later spread to the United States. In 1951, the now professional company presented a command performance before the then Princess Elizabeth (now Queen Elizabeth II). Following the second visit of Queen Elizabeth, the company was granted the title of Royal Winnipeg Ballet in 1953, achieving the distinction of being the first company awarded the British Royal imprimatur. In summer 1964 the company made its United States debut in Boston.

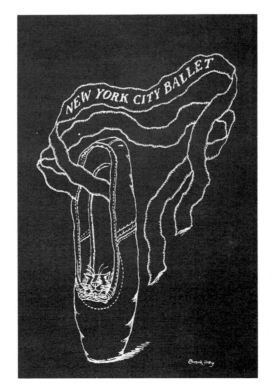

Right: The Royal Winnipeg Ballet's appropriately pastel-hued poster, announcing their spring 1978 New York season. A pair of over-sized toe shoes poised gently on an open tulip, designed by Stefan Czernecki.

Left: Edward Gorey's ballet slipper design for the New York City Ballet.

Los Indianos

Describing itself as a "gaucho folk ballet," Los Indianos is an ensemble of nine dancers and five musicians who started working together in Paris in 1972. In addition to presenting traditional folk dances, which include the *Chacarcera, Escondido, El Gato, Valse Criolla, Mediacana, Palito* and *Huella,* it also performs more fanciful, abstract dream sequences, choreographed saber contests, realistic street scenes and, as an exciting finale, a display of gaucho *boleadores.*

When only a year old, the company had already performed at the London Palladium and on Paris television. By 1974, Los Indianos had made appearances at Paris' Olympia Theater, at the opening of the Palais des Congrès, at the Eiffel Tower and, for almost a year, at the Lido. Since 1975, it has presented dances at festivals and performing-arts centers throughout Europe and North Africa. The troupe has twice been featured at the Casino de Monte Carlo and has had four return engagements at the Municipal Casino in Cannes. In 1976, Los Indianos filmed four European television specials. In 1977 the company performed with the Big Apple Circus in New York, and the following year as part of New York's Lincoln Center Out of Doors.

Right: Serapes serve as flying carpets for members of the Los Indianos Gaucho Ballet as they glide above the arid expanses of the Argentine pampas. Below the apt words "Choreographic Visions of South America," the eight floating figures appear to scan the hot, orange terrain for ideas to dance. The caption is printed in three languages across the top of the poster for the international touring company. This poster was designed by Hector Católica in 1977.

LOS INDIANOS

visions chorégraphiques d'amérique latine   choreographic visions of south america   visiones coreográficas de américa latina

American Ballet Theatre

Since American Ballet Theatre was established in 1939, the company has endeavored to build a repertory of the finest ballets in existence and to support the work of developing, gifted choreographers. To date, American Ballet Theatre possesses a repertory that includes many of the "great" 19th-century ballets, outstanding works from the beginning of the 20th century and dances by every contemporary choreographer of note. Of its approximately eighty dancers from all over the world, all are able to perform the varied works with skill and vigor. Principal dancers include Fernando Bujones, Anthony Dowell, Cynthia Gregory, Gelsey Kirkland, Natalia Makarova, John Meehan, Alexander Minz, Marcos Paredes, Kirk Peterson, Marianna Tcherkassky and Martine van Hamel.

American Ballet Theatre not only tours the United States every year, but claims the distinction of being the only major American company to do so. In addition, the ABT has performed in more than fifteen international tours, including those sponsored by the U.S. State Department. In 1960, with State Department support, ABT made its first appearances in the Soviet Union, becoming the first American dance company ever to perform there. The company returned to the Soviet Union in 1966. In 1977 ABT appeared in London, representing the United States in honoring the Queen's Silver Jubilee.

Since 1971, American Ballet Theatre has been the official company of the John F. Kennedy Center for the Performing Arts in Washington, D.C., appearing there many times each year. In New York, the Metropolitan Opera House became ABT's official home in 1977. American Ballet Theatre is directed by Lucia Chase and Oliver Smith.

Since the dancer in motion — leaping, balancing, turning — provides the graphic artist with such visually stunning material, it is easy to understand why most dance posters focus on a body in motion. But dance as a theater experience encompasses many elements, among them costume, set and lighting designs. The following three American Ballet Theatre posters display a range in subject matter, including a poster that features one aspect of dance production, the costuming, and two that highlight a Ballet Theatre star in a breathtaking moment.

Right: Encore! announces ABT's return to the Metropolitan Opera House with Gelsey Kirkland's flying leap in *Don Quixote*, 1978.

Far left: Unlike the other American Ballet Theatre posters pictured here which capture an American Ballet Theatre star in performance, this poster by English designer/painter Oliver Messell highlights an aspect of production—costuming. Messell designed this costume for American Ballet Theatre's 1976 production of *The Sleeping Beauty*.

Left: Her back curving into an extreme arch, Cynthia Gregory sails across this *Swan Lake* poster, 1977.

Encore!

The Murray Louis Dance Company

By the time the Murray Louis Dance Company celebrated its twenty-fifth anniversary in 1978, it had earned a reputation the world over. This mobile company has toured the United States from coast to coast, Canada, Central and South America and such faraway places as India. Reaching ever-broader audiences, the company has been seen on television internationally in Director Murray Louis' five-part educational program *Dance as an Art Form,* as well as in filmed choreographed dances.

Louis began his career as a dancer/choreographer at the Henry Street Playhouse in New York City, where he was lead dancer with the Alwin Nikolais Dance Theatre. By the end of the 1960s, Louis had relinquished that role and was engrossed in the activities of his own company. It was at this time that the Murray Louis Dance Company took part in launching a Title 3 Project with the U.S. Office of Education and the National Endowment for the Arts. Under this program, the company taught and performed in schools all over the United States. When the program became Operation Impact and later the much-lauded Artists in Schools Program, the Murray Louis Dance Company continued to take an active role. An integral part of the American dance scene, the Murray Louis Dance Company was sent by the U.S. State Department to India at this time and also received its first choreographic grant from the National Endowment for the Arts.

In 1970, Louis received a coveted invitation to choreograph and direct the Coty Fashion Award Ceremony in New York City. Also that year, he and Alwin Nikolais moved from the Henry Street Settlement Playhouse to the Space for Innovative Development in midtown Manhattan, and the Chimera Foundation for Dance, Inc., became the home for both the Louis and the Nikolais companies and school.

Possessing a reputation as an international choreographer, Louis has choreographed or set existing works at the Berlin Opera Ballet, the Royal Danish Ballet and the Scottish Ballet, with Rudolf Nureyev. Nureyev later performed Louis' *Moments* with the Murray Louis Dance Company twice on Broadway. In honor of its twenty-fifth year, the company staged the initial segment of Louis' *Glances* on the Public Broadcast Service, set to music of the same name by jazz composer Dave Brubeck.

The company has appeared at the Spoleto Festival in Italy, and Louis himself has received the Critics Award at the International Festival of Weisbaden, Germany; two John Simon Guggenheim Fellowships and the 1977 *Dancemagazine* Award.

Right: Appearing jet-propelled and generating red-hot trailers of energy behind him, choreographer Murray Louis soars across this simple yet highly charged poster by David Byrd.

Left: Attentive and alert, the obscured figure on this stark black-and-white poster readies himself for immediate action. Designed by Charles Fuhrman. Photograph by Steve Winber.

James Cunningham and the Acme Co.

A native of Toronto, Canada, James Cunningham studied and performed as both an actor and a dancer before coming to New York in 1965. After winning honors degrees in English Literature and Drama at the University of Toronto, Cunningham traveled to England, where he furthered his acting, voice, dance and directing studies at the London Academy of Dramatic Arts. Upon his arrival in the United States, he added yoga, tai chi and further dance training to this roster of accomplishments. At the same time he continued to perform as both an actor and a dancer.

Cunningham has taught at a number of colleges and universities, often as a recipient of artist-in-residence grants. He choreographed the movement for stagings of *Twelfth Night* and *Don Giovanni* at the Stratford (Ontario) Shakespeare Festival and has choreographed García Lorca's *Yerma* for Canadian television — as well as writing, choreographing and performing his own productions. The inventive Cunningham has conceived of and actualized numerous pieces for performing areas ranging in diversity from the traditional proscenium theater to the steps of the U.S. Treasury Building on Wall Street in New York. His company, James Cunningham and the Acme Company, celebrated its tenth birthday in 1978 with a retrospective entitled *Mr. Fox Asleep.* Many of Mr. Cunningham's works have been conceived for performance by the company and as many as one hundred fifty volunteer dancing and nondancing performers.

Cunningham's posters are posed studio compositions, and they contain characters from his *Aesop's Fables* and *Everybody in Bed.* The black-and-white poster illustrates a zaniness and sense of the absurd. Through coy humor they illustrate Cunningham's interest in the part of us that is both male and female and in mythological creatures that are both human and animal.

Right: A trio of characters from Cunningham's *Aesop's Fables* pose playfully in this photograph by Jack Mitchell.

Above: Black-and-white T-shirts with red trim are printed with a gathering of animals that lean, perch and crawl on the Acme Company "A." The Latin reads, "What are you doing after the show?"

Left: Poster created from a photograph by Joel Gordon: two dancers in padded nightclothes and masks fashioned into exaggerated old people's faces—wrinkled and sagging—approach each other gingerly in Cunningham's *Everybody in Bed*, which premiered in 1973.

James Cunningham
AND
the Acme Dance Co.

Capezio Ballet Makers

For over ninety years, Capezio Ballet Makers has been shoeing and dressing dancers and theater people. After coming from Italy to the United States in 1887, Salvatore Capezio set up a small cobbler's shop near the old Metropolitan Opera House. An appreciator of all the arts, Capezio especially loved the dance. It was his dancer wife (who first introduced him to the legendary Anna Pavlova) for whom he was later to construct dancing slippers. In time, his store became a gathering place for famous dancers, actors and actresses of the era. Over the years, in addition to manufacturing dance shoes, Capezio expanded to produce a myriad of other performance-related practice clothing and costumes.

Capezio services the dance world in other ways, too. Each year since 1952, the Capezio Foundation has bestowed the Capezio Dance Award, whose aim has been to bring new developments in dance to the attention of the general public. This award is presented to people who have made some sort of lasting contribution to the dance world. The award is not confined to one calendar year, nor does it concern itself with recognizing a single "best" work — performance or otherwise — in that span of time. In dance critic John Martin's words, a cash prize is given with the belief that "money given to an artist or a creative worker . . . inevitably contributes to the art itself, where it functions actively to breed further progress worthy of further honors in a lively continuity of growth."

The winners of the Capezio Award have included: S. Hurok, Martha Graham, José Limón, Agnes de Mille, Arthur Mitchell, Robert Joffrey, Jerome Robbins and Merce Cunningham.

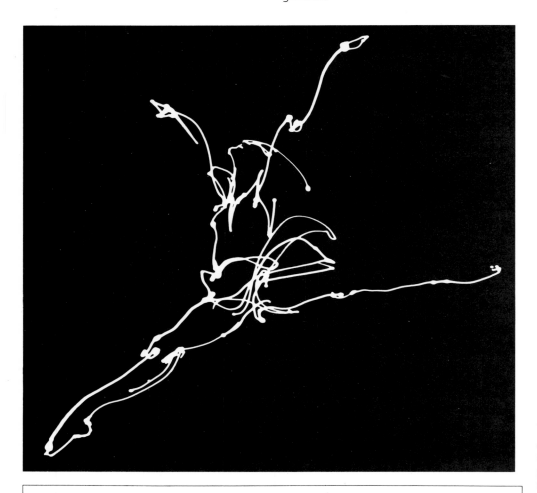

Right: Three dancers pose in Capezio dancewear most becoming and appropriate for their dancing needs. The three dance disciplines illustrated are jazz, modern and ballet. Photographed by Susan Cook.

Above left: The soaring split leap, shown in black-and-white, is the familiar Capezio logo.

Left: This bumper sticker from Capezio Ballet Makers says it all!

Capezio's been dancing since 1887.

Ballet Hispanico

New York's Ballet Hispanico uses movement to illustrate the experience of being a Spanish-speaking American. Its repertory is based in the classical flamenco technique, Latin American folk traditions, the ceremony of the church and the rites of island witchcraft and magic. Modern and jazz works by Alvin Ailey, Talley Beatty and Louis Johnson enrich its offerings.

In the short time since its founding, by Artistic Director Tina Ramirez, in 1970, Ballet Hispanico has staged three New York seasons, has toured the West Coast with assistance from the National Endowment for the Arts Dance Touring Program and in January 1979 embarked on its first European tour. Not only has the company played in the best-known and some of the most sophisticated theaters in this country — in the Kennedy Center for the Performing Arts, the Brooklyn Academy of Music and the Detroit Institute and as part of the Lincoln Center Out of Doors program — but it also tours schools, churches, prisons, community centers and the streets and parks in Spanish-speaking neighborhoods.

Many of the present company members began training with Ms. Ramirez in free and low-cost dance classes she organized in New York's Latin communities, such as the South Bronx. Ramirez' dancers receive rigorous training in flamenco, ballet and modern dance techniques. In addition to the senior performing company, Ballet Hispanico has a junior non-professional company and a children's company.

Right: Four powerful hands clasping castanets shoot up like flames from the bottom of Julio de Diego's bold Latin-style poster.

Left: Tom Caravaglia has caught the sweep of this dancer's flaring skirt as she reaches luxuriously overhead. Behind her, her partner is caught by the photographer as he arches deeply to the side. Mr. Caravaglia has extended the flow of movement into the curve of the words "Ballet Hispanico of New York."

BALLET HISPANICO OF NEW YORK

This project was made possible in part through funds from the National Endowment for the Arts.

The José Limón Dance Company

Born in Mexico in 1908, José Limón began to study dance after sheer accident brought him to a concert by Harald Kreutzberg in 1928. His first teachers were Doris Humphrey and Charles Weidman, and in 1930 he performed in Norman Bel Geddes' Broadway production of *Lysistrata,* for which his teachers had staged the incidental dances and finale. In time, Limón began to perform with the Humphrey-Weidman Company and to choreograph, mainly trios and duets. By 1937 he was choreographing large group pieces, many of which dealt with Mexican and Spanish themes. Following service in the Army from 1943 to 1945, Limón set out, with Doris Humphrey's assistance, to establish his own company in 1946. His *Choreographic Offering* was created as a dance tribute to Ms. Humphrey and her style of movement, out of which his own work had developed. Among the sixty-nine works he choreographed in his lifetime, *The Moor's Pavane* has become a classic, performed the world over by both ballet and modern dance companies.

Though Limón died in 1972, his work is in the repertory of numerous companies, and it continues to be appreciated for its grace and strength. But perhaps the greatest tribute to the power of Limón's choreography is that the Limón Company survives — becoming the first major American dance company to continue after its founder's death.

One of the oldest dance companies in the United States, the José Limón Dance Company made its New York debut in January 1947 at the Belasco Theater. Since then, it has toured twenty-nine foreign countries and forty-three of the American states. In 1954 the Limón Company launched the Cultural Exchange Program of the U.S. State Department by touring South America, and under State Department auspices it has also visited Europe (1957), South and Central America (1960), the Far East (1963) and the Soviet Union (1973).

Dancers who have performed with the company include Ruth Currier, Betty Jones, Lucas Hoving and guest artist Pauline Koner. Following Limón's

death, Daniel Lewis became acting Artistic Director. In August 1973 the company presented its first performances under Ruth Currier at the American Dance Festival, with which it has been connected since the initial festival in summer 1948. In February 1974 the company presented a season —its first since Mr. Limón's death—at City Center Downstairs.

In June 1974, the Limón Company was invited to become the resident dance company of the 92nd Street YM-YWHA, which had nurtured many of the outstanding modern dance choreographers of the '30s and '40s, including Doris Humphrey, Charles Weidman and Helen Tamiris. The Limón Company remained as Company in Residence until June 1978. Under the artistic direction of Limón dancer Carla Maxwell, the company has evolved into a repertory ensemble, performing the works of Limón, Humphrey, Murray Louis, Lucas Hoving and Pauline Koner.

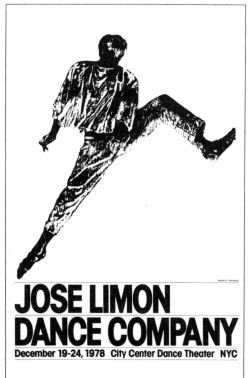

Right: A compellingly direct poster by Gilbert Lesser which announces the Limón Company's thirtieth anniversary in 1976. The word "Limon" and a vibrant red arched foot make the statement: *Limón dance!*

Far left: An austere yet elegant black-and-white poster that shows one of the stained-glass windows at the Cathedral Church of St. John the Divine in New York, where the José Limón Dance Company presented its spring 1978 season. The works were carefully chosen to best suit the Gothic styling of the cathedral, the largest in the world, and included *Choreographic Offering, The Moor's Pavane* and *Missa Brevis.*

Left: Typifying the abounding vitality and strength of Limón's choreography, this manly dancer conquers the air he occupies. A woodcut by Carla Bauer.

limón

José Limón
Dance Company
Thirtieth
Anniversary
1946-1976

GILBERT LESSER

The New York City Ballet

Unlike any other arts organization in the United States, the New York City Ballet trains its own dancers, creates its own dances and appears in its own theater. And it is the only ballet company in the world to claim two permanent homes — the New York State Theater and the Saratoga Performing Arts Center in upstate New York. The New York City Ballet was conceived by Lincoln Kirstein, who dreamed of fashioning a company of American artists rather than imported performers. Kirstein knew that the initial step in developing such an organization would be a school where young American artists could study with the greatest ballet master available.

When Lincoln Kirstein met George Balanchine in London in 1933, he knew he had discovered the perfect person to help him launch his ballet company. Balanchine had been schooled in the tradition of the Russian ballet and had joined the renowned Diaghilev company as a choreographer at the young age of 20. Kirstein invited Balanchine to come to America to establish a school which would prepare the dancers for his American ballet.

The years that followed were not without disappointments, nor were they easy. The debut performance of the school's students, outdoors, had to be canceled because of rain. When both its manager and its finances collapsed, the first tour of the still-new American Ballet had to be called off. Shortly thereafter, a three-year

residence with the Metropolitan Opera as its official ballet company was terminated following a dispute. Many more companies were formed and dissolved. During World War II, Kirstein spent time in the Army while Balanchine choreographed for the Ballet Russe de Monte Carlo. Through all this the school survived.

Following the war, they rented New York's City Center Theater, and Kirstein and Balanchine started the Ballet Society. It was at this time that Morton Baum, then Chairman of the City Center's Finance Committee, suggested to Kirstein that he change the ensemble into a New York City Ballet — and he did.

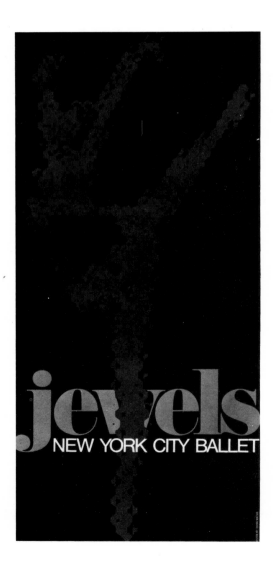

Right: The charming design for this New York City Ballet poster by Edward Gorey appears also on T-shirts, tote bags and New York City Ballet Boutique bags.

Far left: Jewels, a group of ballets choreographed by George Balanchine, premiered in April 1967. Consisting of three sections titled "Rubies," "Emeralds" and "Diamonds," the work was inspired when Balanchine visited the exclusive New York jewelry store Van Cleef & Arpels. Against a black background, rich gem-colored squares define the shape of a dancer. The jagged outlines of the figures suggest the multifaceted, sparkling effect of precious gems.

Left: Edward Gorey's designs for a series of buttons promoting the New York City Ballet.

NEW

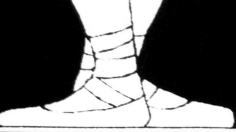

YORK

CITY

BALLET

Edward Gorey

The New York City Ballet *(continued)*

Since 1948, the company has been part of New York's City Center of Music and Drama. It currently performs twenty-three weeks of the year in the New York State Theater, which it opened in 1964 as its resident ballet company, and spends its summers in Saratoga, New York, at the Performing Arts Center there. With more than twenty international engagements to its credit, the company has appeared in every country in Europe except Norway and in Japan, the Philippines and Australia. The New York City Ballet has traveled to the Soviet Union twice, and to several of the largest cities in the United States and Canada. As the largest American dance institution, the company claims ninety-five dancers and an active repertory of over seventy-five works, many of which have been choreographed by George Balanchine and Jerome Robbins. The School of American Ballet, the official school of the New York City Ballet, is located in the Juilliard building at Lincoln Center, and it has a student body of over three hundred fifty dancers from all over the United States.

DYBBUK·

NEW YORK CITY BALLET

Right: A dignified poster features a lyre against a muted blue-green background, to celebrate the New York City Ballet's Stravinsky Festival. In just one week, June 18 to 25, 1972, the company staged the premieres of twenty-two new works to Stravinsky's music.

Left: Jerome Robbins' *Dybbuk,* which had its premiere in 1974 as *Dybbuk Variations,* uses S. Ansky's 1920 Yiddish play *The Dybbuk* as its source. Of Central European derivation, the dybbuk is a spirit of one person that inhabits the body of another person. The score, by Leonard Bernstein, was developed from the numerology of the Cabala. Black and white make a powerful combination on this forbidding poster, designed by Rouben Ter-Arutunian, of sacred Hebrew characters encased in the center of a labyrinth.

City Center of Music & Drama, Inc. presents
new york city ballet
STRAVINSKY FESTIVAL
June 18th to 25th, 1972
DONN MATUS

The Alvin Ailey American Dance Theater

Ever since 1972, when the New York City Ballet presented the all-Stravinsky festival honoring that composer, Ailey had wanted to stage a tribute to Duke Ellington. It was Ailey's wish to honor Ellington while he was still alive, but money and scheduling problems prohibited Ailey from realizing the idea until America's Bicentennial year, two years after Ellington's death. The week-long "Ailey Celebrates Ellington" festival consisted of dances both old and new that Ailey had choreographed to Ellington scores.

Included in the tribute was the jazzy, playful *pas de 'Duke,'* which teamed up ballet star Mikhail Baryshnikov (5'4", costumed in white satin) with Alvin Ailey Dance Theater's Judith

Jamison (5'8", costumed in black satin). The story goes that Baryshnikov had seen the Ailey Company on its 1969 tour in Leningrad, was intrigued by its combination of modern and jazz dance and was eager to try it.

Alvin Ailey, who had danced with Lester Horton in Los Angeles, where he grew up, and with Martha Graham, Hanya Holm, Doris Humphrey and Charles Weidman in New York, formed his first company, the Alvin Ailey Dance Theater, in 1957. Taking advantage of its interracial composition, the U.S. State Department sponsored tours of the company in the Far East and Russia. The company has also visited Europe many times, appearing at the Edinburgh

Festival in 1968. Ailey's work appears in the repertory of the Joffrey Ballet, American Ballet Theater and the Harkness Ballet. Ailey choreographed the dance sequences in Samuel Barber's *Antony and Cleopatra,* which opened the new Metropolitan Opera House at Lincoln Center in 1966, and was invited to perform at the Kennedy Center in Washington, D.C. for the performing arts Inaugural Eve tribute to President Jimmy Carter in 1977.

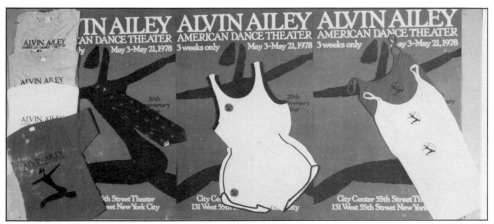

Right: As cool as Ellington's jazz and as clean and sharp as Ailey's choreography, the red, white and blue '30s-style poster was designed by Bea Feitler for Ailey's tribute to Duke Ellington.

Above: The effective *pas de 'Duke'* poster was designed by Michael Wollman.

Left: Michael Hampton's black figure streaks across Alvin Ailey's posters, buttons, T-shirts, tank tops, trunks and ties, announcing the company's twentieth year. The display, mounted by the Friends of Alvin Ailey, hung in the City Center Theater gallery during spring 1978.

Ailey
Celebrates
Ellington

Alvin Ailey City Center Dance Theater

at the New York State Theater
Lincoln Center

Aug. 10-22, 1976
Two weeks

design by Beau Fischer

The San Francisco Ballet Company

San Francisco Ballet dancer Gary Wahl slices through the air, muscles taut, defending himself against an unseen enemy, in *Shinju*. Choreographed in 1975 by Company Director Michael Smuin, *Shinju* is a compelling Kabuki-style dance drama, rooted in ancient legends, by the Japanese dramatist Chikamatsu. In this dance tragedy, two ill-fated lovers commit *shinju,* or double suicide. In the ballet, dedicated to Smuin's wife, *Shinju* cast member Paula Tracy, Smuin skillfully and tastefully merges Eastern and Western movement styles, combining the intricacies of classical ballet vocabulary with the pauses, silences and stillnesses characteristic of Bunraku and Kabuki.

The San Francisco Ballet, America's oldest ballet company, was established in 1933 as the San Francisco Opera Ballet. This venerable company claims a number of other firsts: the San Francisco Ballet was the first ballet company in the United States to stage many of the full-length classics, such as *Coppelia, Swan Lake* and *The Nutcracker.* The company also possesses an established school, which has trained some of America's leading ballet stars, such as Cynthia Gregory.

Much of the San Francisco Ballet's longevity can be attributed to the dedication of the dancers and to community support. In 1974, when the company was close to folding because of lack of funds, the dancers themselves mounted a "do-or-die" campaign to "Save Our Ballet." They performed in store windows, danced during half time at a San Francisco 49ers football game and manned telephones to raise funds to keep the company afloat. They succeeded. San Franciscans rallied to the cause, showing their "ballet buttons" and bumper stickers and contributing the necessary financial support to keep the company going.

show me your ballet button.
san francisco ballet booster.

Guest Artists
Valery & Galina Panov

San Francisco Ballet

Right: A soft-hued *Nutcracker* poster is illustrated by Judy Clifford and designed by Artworks.

Above: San Francisco Ballet bumper sticker used by permission of San Francisco Ballet. Design and copy courtesy San Francisco Newspaper Agency; Sandy Thompson, designer.

Left: Gary Wahl points a strong, straight leg as fiercely as his spear in the ballet *Shinju.*

Lew Christensen's   Spectacular Production

Nutcracker

December 10 through 26, Opera House San Francisco / Tickets on sale Monday, November 15, Opera Box Office,
(415) 431-1210 and most Bay Area ticket agencies.   San Francisco Ballet. Directors: Lew Christensen, Michael Smuin.

The Nutcracker

A holiday favorite the world over, *The Nutcracker* was first produced at the Maryinsky Theatre, St. Petersburg, December 19, 1892. For this ballet, consisting of two acts and three scenes, the choreography and book were by Lev Ivanov to Peter Tchaikovsky's score; the decor was by M. I. Botcharov.

Antonietta Dell-Era and Paul Gerdt performed the roles of the Sugar Plum Fairy and the Cavalier. This Christmas tale, which is based on one of the well-known stories of E. T. A. Hoffmann, relates the adventures of a little girl, Clara, who receives a nutcracker in the form of a soldier as a holiday present from a mysterious old man, Herr Drosselmeyer. When she falls asleep after the Christmas party, Clara dreams that she sees a battle between the gifts — a battalion of lead soldiers — and some mice! In her dream, the Nutcracker fights the King of the Mice, and Clara rescues the Nutcracker by hurling her shoe at the Mouse King. At that moment, the Nutcracker turns into a prince, who takes Clara away to the Land of the Snowflakes, Konfiturenburg, the domain of the Sugar Plum Fairy.

In 1934, under its French title of *Casse-Noisette,* *The Nutcracker* was restaged by Nicholas Sergeyev for the "Vic-Wells" (later Sadler's Wells and now Royal Ballet), Sadler's Wells Theatre, London. Alicia Markova and Harold Turner performed in the principal roles, and the Sugar Plum Fairy was later danced by Mary Honer, Margot Fonteyn, Nadia Nerina and many others, often partnered by Robert Helpmann.

This seasonal offering was in the repertory of the Markova-Dolin Ballet, and other versions are or were staged by many other companies, including the Ballet Russe de Monte Carlo, the National Ballet of Canada and Ballet Rambert. The London Festival Ballet revived *The Nutcracker* with Alicia Markova and Anton Dolin in 1950 and seven years later developed a yet newer version by David Lichine and supervised by Alexandre Benois. It was presented at Festival Hall, London, Christmas Eve, 1957. Nathalie Krassovska and Jon Gilpin danced the Sugar Plum Fairy and the Cavalier, whose *pas de deux* from the Ivanov original is an excerpt often performed by many companies and groups.

The New York City Ballet Nutcracker

In the first performance of this New York City Ballet version, choreographed by George Balanchine in 1954, Maria Tallchief and Nicholas Magallanes performed the coveted roles of the Sugar Plum Fairy and the Cavalier. Though differing somewhat from the original Ivanov version, the Balanchine *Nutcracker* is still presented in two acts and three scenes. In its yearly, much anticipated one-month run, New Yorkers flock to see this holiday attraction, complete with the Christmas tree that grows taller and taller, the battle between mice and lead soldiers, and a bed that travels into a forest where snowflakes dance. In 1964, Rouben Ter-Arutunian redesigned the decor and sets, which were originally created by Horace Armistead and Barbara Karinska. Like the other two versions of *The Nutcracker,* Balanchine's is set to Peter Tchaikovsky's score.

Right: An Oriental flavor pervades this poster for the Royal Winnipeg Ballet *Nutcracker.* Designer Stefan Czernecki portrays a smartly and colorfully uniformed Nutcracker with an exaggerated nose, bulging eye and pink face that suggest an Oriental theater mask.

Left: In this poster, designed by Donn Matus for the New York City Ballet, Herr Drosselmeyer waves Clara's gift, the nutcracker, above his head.

ROYAL WINNIPEG BALLET
director/directeur ARNOLD SPOHR

NUTCRACKER
choreography JOHN NEUMEIER
music TCHAIKOVSKY

The Pennsylvania Ballet

Founded in 1963 by Barbara Weisberger, who now functions as Company Director, and Benjamin Harkarvy, who serves as Artistic Director, the Pennsylvania Ballet is composed of thirty-two dancers. Working as an ensemble group, it aspires, in its own words, toward "stylistic perfection and homogeneity of performance," while at the same time encouraging the evolution of the art of choreography.

The Pennsylvania Ballet performs a diversity of works, including those of Balanchine, Butler, Tudor, Limón, Harkarvy, Van Manen, Robbins, Taylor, Petipa and Fokine, among others. The group divides its repertory into three categories: 19th- and 20th-century classic works, which use the impressive size of the company to its best advantage; dances choreographed by contemporary choreographers and works created specially for the Pennsylvania Ballet, which the company looks upon as invaluable to the development of its future.

In performance the greater part of the year, the Pennsylvania Ballet has toured in thirty-five states and in Canada. During residencies in the communities where it is appearing, the company stages, in addition to concerts, lecture-demonstrations, master classes and specially oriented classes and presentations for schools, colleges and local groups. In its own home of Philadelphia, the Pennsylvania Ballet makes its base for four series at the Shubert Theatre, plus presenting twenty performances of *The Nutcracker* at the Academy of Music. It is also the resident ballet company of the Brooklyn Academy of Music in New York, where it presents a fall and a spring season.

The school of the Pennsylvania Ballet, also located in Philadelphia, preceded the formation of the company by a year. As its main program, the school offers classes for professionally oriented students at the elementary, intermediate and advanced levels. For outstanding students, it has a scholarship program and, for preprofessional students, an Apprentice Program. This program lasts for two years and is an intensive preparation for possible eventual inclusion into the company itself. The Apprentice Program strengthens the company by enabling it to train its own dancers.

Right: This poster for the Pennsylvania Ballet was created by Alexander Calder. Margo Sappington choreographed the ballet *Under the Sun* as a tribute to Calder. The ballet had its premiere in 1976 to a specially commissioned score by Michael Kamens.

"Under the Sun"
a tribute in dance to
ALEXANDER CALDER
World Premiere October 6, 1976

Pennsylvania
Ballet

Dancemagazine

For over fifty years, *Dancemagazine* has served as the undisputed leading periodical for the American dance community, *Dancemagazine* evolved from the merging of two forerunners — *American Dancer,* first published in 1927 as a monthly magazine and the official publication of the Dancing Masters of America, and a magazine called *Dance.* In 1942, Rudolf Orthwine purchased both periodicals and published them together as *Dance.* Six years later he changed the name to *Dancemagazine* and included news, features, reviews and interviews related to this burgeoning American art—dance. With an international circulation, *Dancemagazine* has been awarded numerous prizes for design and printing. *Dancemagazine* is the only dance publication indexed in *Reader's Guide to Periodical Literature*, and it is frequently reprinted in foreign languages by the U.S. Information Service for special promotion abroad.

The covers shown here reflect the magazine's ability to combine topicality with graphic excellence.

Right: October 1978, Clive Thompson; photo by Herbert Migdoll.

Left: June 1974, Frederic Franklin; photo by Constantine.

Dancer
zine

Anniversaries:
Ailey's
20th
Humphrey/
Weidman's
50th

Chicago's
International
Ballet
Festival

Akron's
Ohio
Ballet

October
1978
$2.00

Clive Thompson

The Houston Ballet

The Houston Ballet was established in 1955 in Houston, Texas, and during its early years appeared with the Houston Symphony and the Houston Grand Opera. By 1960, the Houston Ballet had been named the official ballet for the Opera. At this time, the Houston Ballet Foundation supported the dance in general by presenting performances of Houston Ballet Academy students and by hosting professional touring dance companies.

Eleven years after its founding, the group performed with the Houston Grand Opera for the opening of the Jesse H. Jones Hall for the Performing Arts, which eventually would house the Houston Ballet. A year later, the Houston Ballet staged *Giselle,* marking its first presentation of a classic ballet. In 1968, the Houston Ballet Foundation launched an extensive fund-raising campaign to establish a permanent, professional repertory company in the Southwestern United States. By early 1969, the Foundation's Board of Trustees had approved the formation of a performing group consisting of sixteen dancers. In the next four years, the Houston Ballet became an established company, performing throughout the Midwest and Southwest. In 1972, the developing company experienced a landmark year: the Houston Ballet Orchestra was formed to replace taped music; the company expanded from sixteen to thirty dancers, and its season lengthened.

In 1976 Ben Stevenson was appointed Artistic Director. The English-born Stevenson had been a member of the Royal Ballet, a Principal Dancer with the London Festival Ballet and Director of the Chicago Ballet from 1974 to 1976. He had also performed in musical theater and on films and television. Under his direction, the Houston Ballet has concentrated on fortifying the company with dancers from its academy. To accomplish this, the company not only has stopped featuring guest artists, but has expanded its studio facilities to accommodate its doubled enrollment.

The Houston Ballet, which has received support from the Ford Foundation, made its New York debut in 1978 and its international debut in Guanajuato, Mexico, when it opened the Sixth Festival Internacional Cervantino with two performances of *Swan Lake* at the Teatro Juárez Opera House.

Right: The desert land and skyscapes are illustrated in this poster for *Allen's Landing,* one of the three ballets that make up choreographer James Clauser's *Texas Trilogy.* Doris Hood's design for this poster was taken from the backdrop that hung on stage during the dance.

HOUSTON BALLET ALLEN'S LANDING
1975

Nancy Meehan Dance Company

Nancy Meehan, who danced with the Erick Hawkins Dance Company throughout the '60s, went on to form her own company in 1970. Featuring her choreography exclusively, the company has performed in New York's Central Park Delacorte Theater and at New York University, the American Dance Festival and the Theater of the Riverside Church. In 1976, Nancy Meehan received a Guggenheim Fellowship for Choreography. Presenting dances that are devoid of elaborate costumes or sets, Ms. Meehan attempts to use movement itself to create, in her words, "dances using natural imagery as metaphor for states of being and/or mind."

Right and left: For the concert announcements on these pages, painter Anthony Candido has created all of the Nancy Meehan Company's graphics using Chinese ink and brush.

Nancy Meehan
Dance Co.

"...she is one of the
major & most serious
Talents in the modern dance."
—Anna Kisselgoff, N.Y. Times

NEW YORK UNIVERSITY THEATRE. 35 WEST 4th STREET
(EAST OF WASHINGTON SQUARE)
APRIL 13, 14, 15 & 16 at 8:00 P.M.
GENERAL ADMISSION $4.00 · TDF + $1.50
RESERVATIONS 598-3067

THESE CONCERTS ARE PARTIALLY FUNDED BY THE N.Y.S.C.A.

The Feld Ballet

The Feld Ballet made its debut in May 1974 at the Newman Theater at the Public Theater complex of the New York Shakespeare Festival. What was to have been a three-week season was extended to five weeks and featured a six-ballet repertory. During its second Public Theater season, the company performed its first work by Glen Tetley, guest choreographer, *Embrace Tiger and Return to Mountain,* and Eliot Feld's *The Real Mc Coy* set to a Gershwin score was given its premiere. The company's fall 1975 New York season included Feld premieres of *Mazurka* and *Excursions* as well as a revival of his famous *Harbinger.* In the spring of 1976, The Feld Ballet was selected the official United States cultural presentation in Latin America for the Bicentennial year. For nine weeks, under the sponsorship of the U.S. State Department, The Feld Ballet toured Mexico and Central and South America.

The company returned to New York and opened its 1976 season at the Public Theater with the premiere of Feld's *Impromptu* to a harp solo by Albert Roussel, and a company New York premiere of *A Soldier's Tale* to the Stravinsky score. Included also in that season were a revival of Feld's *A Poem Forgotten* and the staging of Kathryn Posin's *Waves.* In March 1977 The Feld Ballet moved to "uptown" Manhattan for performances at the City Center 55th Street Dance Theater. Mikhail Baryshnikov performed with the company in a *pas de deux* created especially for him and Christine Sarry by Eliot Feld, *Variations on 'America'* to Ives/Schuman music. Also premiered was Feld's *A Footstep of Air,* choreographed to a Beethoven arrangement of Irish and Scottish folk songs.

The Feld Ballet has performed in twenty-nine of the fifty United States and for capacity audiences in the 2,300-seat opera house in Ottawa's National Arts Centre. The company has performed at Wolf Trap Farm Park in Vienna, Virginia, since 1974; at Jacob's Pillow in Massachusetts; at Artpark in New York State; at Meadowbrook in Detroit; at the first Spoleto Festival USA and at the American Dance Festival in 1978 at Duke University in Durham, North Carolina. In addition to live concert performances, the Feld Ballet has been seen on television on the PBS *Dance for Camera* and *Live from Wolf Trap* and *Dance in America* performing arts series.

In January 1978, at the Shubert Theatre in Los Angeles, The Feld Ballet became the first ballet company to be presented by the Shubert Organization. The company's spring 1978 New York Broadway season also was produced by the Shuberts and Mikhail Baryshnikov performed with the company in Feld's *Santa Fe Saga* set to Morton Gould's score.

The Feld Ballet works out of its own spacious and bright studios in lower Manhattan in 20,000 square feet that before renovation was a belt factory. The associate school of the company, The New Ballet School, was started in January 1978. The New Ballet School is a tuition-free, professional ballet training program for children from New York City public schools. Feld saw city children as an untapped dance and performing arts resource and went to the Board of Education for help in arranging auditions in the schools.

The activities of The New Ballet School are made possible with both public and private funds.

In January 1979, Original Ballets Foundation, Inc., the nonprofit sponsor of The Feld Ballet, took title to the Elgin Theater, a former cinema located at 19th Street and Eighth Avenue in New York City. The Elgin Theater will be converted to a 500-seat modern theater for dance, will provide a permanent home for the Feld Ballet and will be available as a performance space for other dance companies.

Right: Their costumes designed by Willa Kim and appropriately decorated with the Stars and Stripes for the Feld Ballet *Variations on 'America,'* which premiered in 1977 to a score by Charles Ives and William Schuman, Christine Sarry and Mikhail Baryshnikov are caught during a moment of "pretend." Forming make-believe feathers in his hair with one hand and covering his lips for an Indian war whoop with the other, Baryshnikov steals across the stage like a warrior stalking his prey. Christine Sarry, wearing a World War I helmet and aiming an imaginary rifle, perches precariously on the "warrior's" back. From a photo by Herbet Migdoll. Poster designed by Gerry Gentile.

Left: Full of unfinished motion, the dancer leaves us awaiting his next move—up, over, down, or to either side. This figure adorns The Feld Ballet posters, brochures and flyers, available in black and white and in color, and shows choreographer Eliot Feld in *The Real Mc Coy,* which he choreographed in 1974 to music by George Gershwin. Photo by Bert Stern. Poster designed by Gerry Gentile.

PRESENTED BY ORIGINAL BALLETS FOUNDATION, INC.

ELIOT FELD BALLET

CHRISTINE SARRY AND MIKHAIL BARYSHNIKOV IN "VARIATIONS ON AMERICA"

The Luis Rivera Spanish Dance Company

The Luis Rivera Spanish Dance Company was formed by Luis Rivera in 1970. Composed of Spanish dancers, vocalists and instrumentalists, the company has appeared throughout the United States and in such diverse locations as Bermuda, Newfoundland, Denmark, Canada and England. The Luis Rivera Spanish Dance Company made its concert debut at the Jacob's Pillow Dance Festival in Lee, Massachusetts. Its repertory includes a variety of Spanish dances and music, in the flamenco, medieval, regional and classical styles.

Luis Rivera was born in California of Mexican-American ancestry. His first dance training was in Los Angeles with Michael Brigante, Martin Vargas and Luisa Triana. Later he accepted an invitation to dance with the Ballet Espanol Ximénez-Vargas in Spain. At the same time he furthered his flamenco studies, and he did not return to the United States until he performed at the New York World's Fair with Spain's Ballet Lorquiana. Soon after, Luis Rivera was invited to perform with the Jose Greco Company. In only one week he attained the status of Principal Male Dancer, a position he held for three years until he left the company to form his own.

Rivera has made major appearances in London's Royal Festival Hall, the Teatro de Bellas Artes in Mexico City, Madrid's Teatro de la Zarzuela, the Americana Hotel and Chateau Madrid in New York, Caesar's Palace in Las Vegas and the El San Juan in Puerto Rico. He has returned many times to the Jacob's Pillow Dance Festival and to La Meri's Ethnic Dance Festival. To his credit are films made in Hollywood and Madrid, television appearances on the Ed Sullivan and Johnny Carson shows and tours with Alan King, Marlene Dietrich and Frank Sinatra.

Right: On this prize-winning poster for the Luis Rivera Spanish Dance Company, photographer Herbert Migdoll illustrates the contained ferocity of the Spanish dancer as his booted foot descends to the floor. The multiple images create the effect of sound. This poster was awarded first prize in 1978 in the poster division by the Association of College, University and Community Arts Administrators and second prize in the flyer division by the International Society for Performing Arts Administrators. Designed by the Asselin Byars Company.

Luis Rivera

Spanish Dance Company

The Joffrey Ballet

The Joffrey Ballet first performed as the Robert Joffrey Ballet Concert in May 1954 in New York City, and its dances included the premiere of Joffrey's *Pas de Déesses.* Just two years later, the troupe set out on its first tour with a new name — Robert Joffrey's Theatre Dancers — and possessing a repertory of four Joffrey ballets and six dancers. By 1958, the company had changed its name again — to Robert Joffrey Theatre Ballet — and expanded to eight dancers. And once again, two years later, in 1960, now encompassing many dancers and an orchestra, the ballet chose a new name — the Robert Joffrey Ballet.

In 1962, the Robert Joffrey Ballet was asked to appear at the Festival of Two Worlds in Spoleto, Italy, but lacked the funds necessary to cover traveling expenses. Balletomane/philanthropist Rebekah Harkness, hearing of the group's plight, offered to pick up the tab through the Rebekah Harkness Foundation. Robert Joffrey had other plans and asked if the funds could instead be used to pay his dancers during rehearsals prior to their annual tour, something the group had as yet been unable to afford. The Foundation granted Joffrey's request, and in addition it undertook the sponsorship of a summer workshop in Rhode Island, where many choreographers were invited to create new works. In the years that followed, the company performed all over the world — in the Near and Middle East, India, Pakistan, the Soviet Union.

Composed mainly of young dancers, the Robert Joffrey Ballet gained a reputation for youthfulness, vitality and freshness. In addition to Joffrey's own works, the Ballet features works by Gerald Arpino, Brian Macdonald, Alvin Ailey, Twyla Tharp and Agnes de Mille. Though Joffrey's association with the Harkness Foundation ended in 1964 and the company disbanded, Joffrey, undaunted, formed a new company. Aided by a large Ford Foundation grant, the new company made its debut at the Jacob's Pillow Dance Festival in 1965 and its New York debut at Central Park's Delacorte Theater. Following the resounding success of a seven-performance season at the New York City Center Theater, the Joffrey was invited to become the official resident company of the City Center. It was then that the company became the City Center Joffrey Ballet, with Robert Joffrey acting as Artistic Director and Gerald Arpino as principal choreographer and Assistant Director.

Robert Joffrey was born Abdullah Jaffa Anver Bey Khan in Seattle, Washington. He began his dance training there, and later studied in New York at the School of American Ballet, with Alexandra Fedorova, and studied modern dance with May O'Donnell and Gertrude Shurr. His professional dancing career began with Roland Petit's Ballets de Paris. His early choreographic efforts were staged most often with students at the School of Performing Arts in New York, where he taught. Though Robert Joffrey established his own school in 1955 — the American Ballet Center — he has taught in a variety of contexts. He has choreographed for television and for the New York City Opera Company and the Dallas Civic Opera.

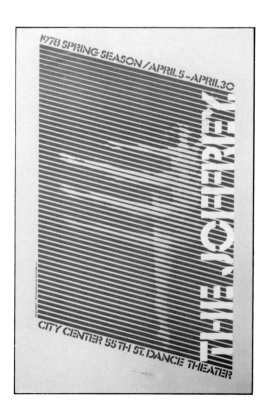

Right: As electric as the dance *Astarte,* pink, green, purple and white dots merge against a dark background on this poster, creating a multiplicity of images, like the afterimages of a strobe light. Robert Joffrey's *Astarte,* featured on the cover of *Time* magazine, was the first mixed-media dance to be staged by a major dance company. *Astarte* had its world premiere in New York City on September 19, 1967, at the City Center, with Maximiliano Zamosa and Trinette Singleton dancing the lead roles. This "psychedelic" ballet began in a then unconventional way. Zamosa, clad in a corduroy jump suit, emerges from the audience, inexorably drawn to Astarte (Ms. Singleton), the goddess of love and fertility, who stands on stage. Her body is covered with wild, swirling paisleys, her head painted with strange designs. Standing before her, Zamosa disrobes and they dance a love duet while their images flash on a huge screen behind them. Crome Syrcus, a rock group, played live accompaniment. Poster by Herbert Migdoll. Photo design by Herbert Migdoll.

Left: Executed in various color combinations, this poster by Herbert Migdoll announces the Joffrey 1977 New York spring season. Photo design by Herbert Migdoll.

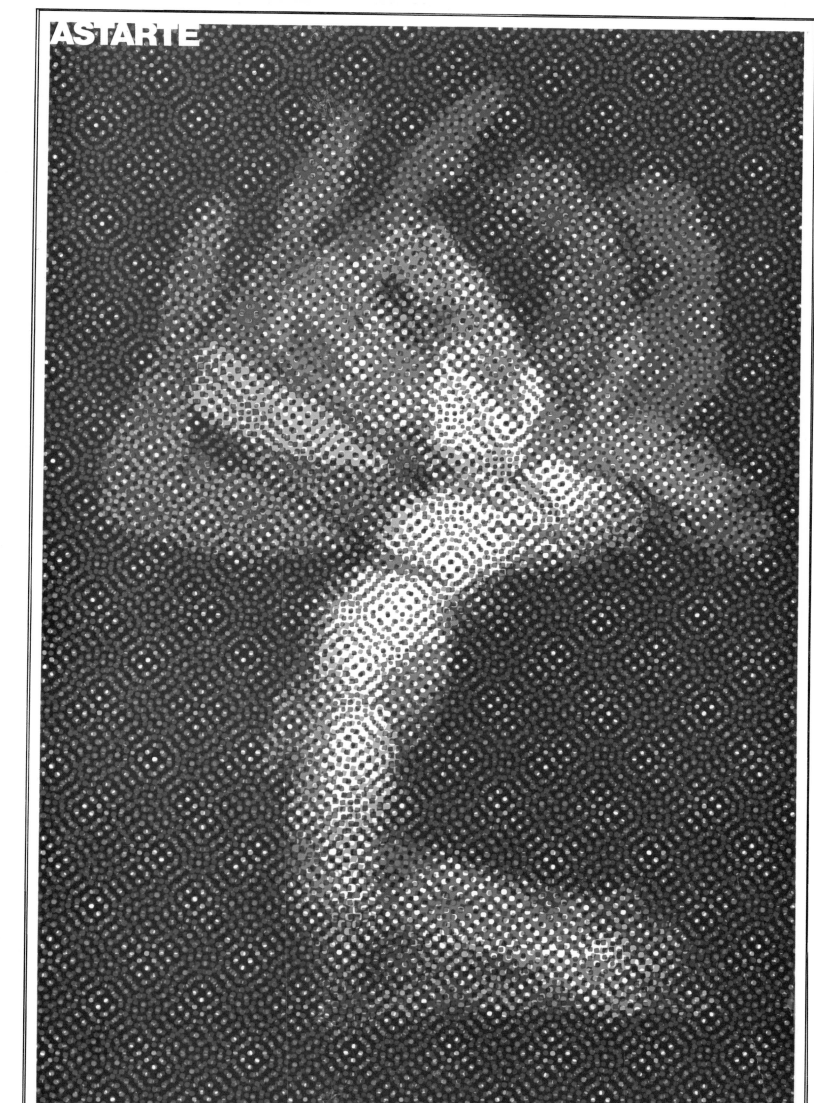

Bella Lewitzky Dance Company

A prime motivator of dance on the West Coast, Bella Lewitzky was born in the California Mojave Desert and received her early dance training with Lester Horton in Los Angeles. She subsequently became Horton's colleague, and together they founded the Dance Theater in Los Angeles, which at that time was one of the few performing arts organizations in this country to have both a school and a performing theater of dance under one roof. In 1951 Ms. Lewitzky established Dance Associates, with a school of modern dance and a performing ensemble. Fifteen years later she formed the Bella Lewitzky Dance Company, which today travels to Europe and throughout the United States as part of the National Endowment for the Arts Dance Touring Program.

Bella Lewitzky has been the recipient of a John Simon Guggenheim Memorial Foundation Fellowship, the annual *Dancemagazine* Award and commissions from the National Endowment for the Arts. She has the distinction of being the nation's only choreographer not based in New York City to receive a major grant for an artistic director's discretionary fund from the Andrew W. Mellon Foundation. Most recently, Ms. Lewitzky's company was presented a special project grant from the CBS Corporation.

Lewitzky has been involved with many organizations contributing to the evolution of dance in the United States. She has served as Dean of the School of Dance, California Institute of the Arts; as Dance Chairman, Idyllwild Arts Foundation, University of Southern California; on the West Coast Executive Board of the Association of American Dance Companies; on the National Advisory Board for Young Audiences and as consultant for the National Humanities Faculty, and she is an Honorary Member of UNESCO's International Dance Association. Ms. Lewitzky has long been involved with the Artists in Schools Program of the National Endowment for the Arts, believing that movement is an essential part of education in learning to solve problems nonverbally.

BELLA LEWITZKY DANCE COMPANY

Right: Designer Rudi Gernreich developed the costume for the Bella Lewitzky Dance Company that connects the two dancers here. Gernreich has chosen to have the dancers "share" a very flexible part of their "costume body" — the spine — which allows great mobility in body facings and movement.

Left: The cutaway, unisex costumes were designed by Rudi Gernreich and complement the dancers' muscled bodies and sleek lines.

Lewitzky

Merce Cunningham Dance Company

Born in the Pacific Northwest in Centralia, Washington, Merce Cunningham first studied movement and theater at the Cornish School in Seattle. By 1953, when he started work with a group of dancers at Black Mountain College in North Carolina, Cunningham had already made many national and international tours as a soloist. Since then, he has choreographed over sixty works for himself and the dancers in his company, which have been seen as far away as the Far and Middle East, Latin America, Australia and Europe and, domestically, in the United States.

Significant to Cunningham's work is that he has joined forces with a number of innovative contemporary artists in other disciplines. In the field of music, John Cage, Earle Brown, Toshi Ichiyanagi and Christian Wolff are but a few of his collaborators. More than forty composers have taken part in the Cunningham company's seventy events in New York City in recent years. Richard Lippold, David Hare, Sonja Sekula, Remy Charlip, Frank Stella, Bruce Nauman, Neil Jenny, Richard Nelson, Mark Lancaster and Cunningham artistic adviser Jasper Johns are some of the painters, sculptors and designers with whom Cunningham has created performance pieces. Cunningham's work has won numerous awards, including the Gold Medal for Choreographic Invention at the Fourth International Festival of the Dance in Paris in 1966 and the Grand Prix at the Belgrade International Theatre Festival, 1972. Cunningham himself has twice received Guggenheim Fellowships for Choreography, the Medal of the Society for the Advancement of Dancing in Sweden in 1964, the New York State Award in 1975 and the Capezio Award in 1977.

Cunningham has both created new works for companies and taught existing works to companies; among them are the New York City Ballet, the Boston Ballet, the Cullberg Ballet in Stockholm and the Theatre du Silence in France. The Merce Cunningham Dance Company was in residence as part of the Avignon Festival and has participated at the Israel Festival, the Athens Festival and the Dubrovnik Festival. In the United States, the company was a resident group at the Brooklyn Academy of Music from 1969 to 1973 and has presented several Broadway seasons. Cunningham has created video works with Charles Atlas and Nam June Paik and has been seen with the company on the *Dance in America* series on Public Broadcast Service.

Right: Morris Graves' *Waning Moon No. 2,* painted in 1943, was chosen by the Merce Cunningham Dance Company in 1977 to announce its Seattle performances of Merce Cunningham's *Inlets.* Symbolforms of the waning moon, one black and white serpent, each with two heads, present an intriguing duality.

Left: Merce Cunningham's soaring figure taken from a brochure designed by John Cage in the mid-fifties.

Cornish Institute Presents

Merce Cunningham and Dance Company

with John Cage

The Lar Lubovitch Dance Company

Often lauded by critics for his ability to successfully merge modern dance and ballet vocabularies, Lubovitch includes both in his own background. He had come to New York from Chicago to study on scholarship at the Juilliard School, where his early training was with such notables as Anthony Tudor, Anna Sokolow, Jóse Limón and members of the Martha Graham Company. In his first year at Juilliard in 1962, he began performing with the Pearl Lang Dance Company, and in the following three years he appeared with the modern dance companies of Donald McKayle and Glen Tetley, among others. By 1965, he was a soloist with the Manhattan Festival Ballet and Principal Dancer and choreographer with the Santa Fe Opera. Only a year after he joined the Harkness Ballet in 1967, Lubovitch took a leave of absence to pursue his own choreographic ideas. In 1969, Lubovitch left the Harkness to form his own company, with which he has been working ever since.

Touring internationally, The Lar Lubovitch Dance Company has appeared at festivals all over the world and at all the major theaters in Sweden, France, Italy, Germany and Canada. Lubovitch himself has also choreographed, performed, taught and lectured on college campuses all over the United States. In addition, his works are included in the repertory of a number of other companies, including American Ballet Theatre, the Royal Danish Ballet, the Alvin Ailey Dance Theater, Ballet Rambert and the National Ballet of Holland.

Right: Artist Ivan Chermayeff of Chermayeff and Geismar Associates sends dancer Christine Wright soaring heavenward through an explosion of vibrant colors on this poster designed for The Lar Lubovitch Dance Company's 1977 New York season. With photographer Louise Gund, Chermayeff has captured the exhilaration and liberation of movement possessed by Lubovitch's dance *Exsultate Jubilate.*

Lar Lubovitch

Dance Company

Dancers

Dancers made its debut at the Royal Poinciana Playhouse in Palm Beach, Florida, on December 21, 1976, following a well-received one-week engagement in New York City in 1975. The dancers who compose this group, which describes itself as a "compact touring-size repertory company," are all classically trained and adept at performing both classical and contemporary ballets. When the company was only six months old, it was chosen to represent the United States in ballet for the twentieth season of the Festival of Two Worlds in Spoleto, Italy. Following this five-week engagement, Dancers appeared at the famous

Jacob's Pillow Dance Festival in Massachusetts. The company staged its first official New York season at the Roundabout Theater in November 1977. Since then, Dancers has toured Florida, the Caribbean, California, Oregon, Washington, Canada and the Midwest. Its broad repertory includes works by Maurice Béjart, Tod Bolender, John Butler, Cliff Keuter, Norman Walker, Rudy Van Danzig, Marcus Schulkind and Leonide Massine, who flew in from Germany to see Dancers' Florida debut.

Dancers is directed by Dennis Wayne, who began performing with his parents' acrobatic act at age 2. He attended the New York School of Performing Arts, where he chose dancing as his career. He went on to study with Norman Walker, May O'Donnell and Paul Sanasardo. He was a soloist with the Harkness Ballet in 1964, and when the company disbanded in 1970, he became a principal dancer with the Joffrey Ballet. Four years later, he joined American Ballet Theatre, where he danced until he left to form Dancers. Not only a dancer, Wayne acted in the film *Summer Wishes, Winter Dreams* with actress Joanne Woodward, an active supporter of Wayne's fledgling company.

Right: A beautiful pastel poster by the French artist Folon.

Above: A ballet slipper and a cowboy boot make an unusual combination on this 1978 poster by Stefan Czernecki for Dancers' Canadian performances.

Left: Calling themselves simply "Dancers," they emblazon the following phrase across advertisements, T-shirts, buttons, Frisbees, key chains and luggage tags: JUST CALL US DANCERS—and even in more than one language!

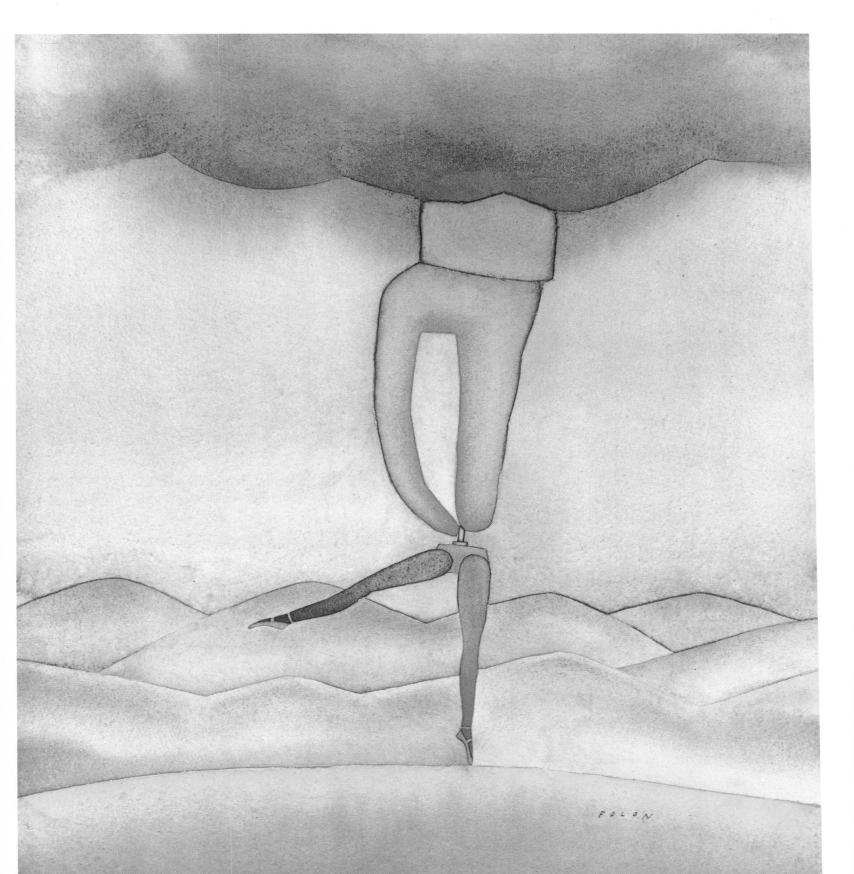

ROUNDABOUT THEATRE NEW YORK NOVEMBER 17 DECEMBER 11

Dancers

Dan Wagoner and Dancers

Company Director Dan Wagoner was born and grew up in the small mountain town of Springfield, West Virginia. His first choreographic efforts took place in the living room of the Wagoner home and included Dan's nine older brothers and sisters. After college and some formal dance training, he first appeared professionally with the Martha Graham Dance Company and later with Paul Taylor.

Since 1971, Dan Wagoner has directed and choreographed for his own company. Possessing a repertory of from eight to ten dances at a time for the company of seven, Dan Wagoner and Dancers has appeared throughout the United States and abroad. Wagoner's dances deal with basic choreographic elements — time, space and energy — and in his own words, "sometimes draw from folk dance or the social dances of the thirties." Poet George Montgomery, who designed the poster below and creates many of the company's graphics, has been a frequent guest performer with Dan Wagoner and Dancers.

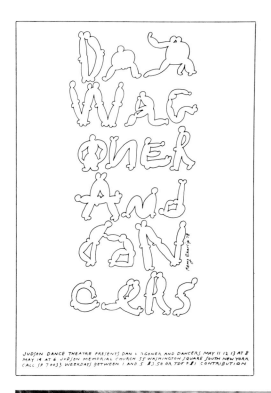

Right: Remy Charlip, theater director, designer, choreographer and dancer in his own right, designed these appealing posters. With feline and canine features recognizable on some, rabbitlike ears on others, the fanciful figures on the Dan Wagoner posters look almost like familiar animals. On this black-and-white poster which you can color in yourself, with their arms outstretched, their flexible bodies leaning, bending, curving, these whimsical creatures seem to be moving through a dance on paper that Charlip has choreographed for them.

Above: The words "Dan Wagoner and Dancers" are spelled out with Charlip's characters on this piece for Wagoner's 1978 concert at the Judson Memorial Church. Placed in various and sundry positions, connected to one another, the figures form a dance of letters.

Left: A magical black-and-white engraving of Adam and Eve in a lush Garden of Eden was designed by poet George Montgomery. Though not representing a specific dance, this piece was chosen for its enchanting flavor, which complemented a duet for a man and a woman Mr. Wagoner was premiering that season.

60

DAN WAGONER AND DANCERS

REMY CHARLIP

The Nikolais Dance Theatre

Alwin Nikolais launched his choreographic career in 1939 in his home state of Connecticut, and just two years later set out on a cross-country tour of the United States with a trio of other dancers who called themselves "Dancers En Route." Since 1967, as Director of the Nikolais Dance Theatre, he has appeared often in the famous theaters and festivals around the world — Europe, the Near East, South and Central America, and the Far East as well as North America. Nikolais, who left home at 15 to become a musician, has a background in painting, acting, directing, designing and lighting. At only 19 he was Director of the Hartford Parks Marionette Theater. It was there, after seeing Mary Wigman perform, that Nikolais began to study dance with a teacher of Wigman technique. He spent his summers attending the dance program at Bennington, Vermont, where he worked with Hanya Holm, Martha Graham, Doris Humphrey, Charles Weidman, José Limón, John Martin and Louis Horst, among others.

Returning from a three-and-one-half-year tour of duty with the Army in 1945, Nikolais focused his dance interests with Hanya Holm. In just a few months he was serving as her assistant, teaching and dancing with her workshop company. After being chosen Director of the Henry Street Playhouse in New York City in 1948, Nikolais began to concentrate on developing his own performance ideas and to form a company. He remained there for twenty-two years, until he left to guide, with Murray Louis, the Louis-Nikolais Dance Theatre and the Louis-Nikolais Dance Theatre Lab, the company's school.

Considered revolutionary in 1951, Nikolais' works were and continue to be abstract rather than psychological, as was the prevailing mode of modern dance then. Multimedia compositions incorporating elaborate and inventive lighting, sound and costuming, his dances are visually as well as kinetically stimulating.

Nikolais' awards have been many. He has been the recipient of two John Simon Guggenheim Memorial Fellowships, as well as ten commissions from the National Endowment for the Arts. His work has been supported by the Ford and Mellon foundations, among other organizations and individuals, including an invitation by the French Government to direct the Centre National de Danse Contemporaine, which involves establishing a school and company in France. His company has appeared on television and film the world over.

Right: So powerfully does this poster capture Alwin Nikolais' phantasmagorical manipulation of color in costuming and lighting and the intriguing shapes and positions he fashions in his dances that the viewer feels he has been brought into the concert hall. Photo by Tom Caravaglia. Design by Roger Merrill.

Nikolais DanceTheatre

Roger Merrill, Graphic Artist: TDAS, Production
Photo: Tom Caravaglia

Andrew deGroat and Dancers

Since 1967, when choreographer and dancer Andrew deGroat presented his first work, *Blanket*, he has collaborated with theater director Robert Wilson in addition to presenting works of his own. DeGroat has choreographed for Wilson's productions *A Letter for Queen Victoria*, at the ANTA Theatre on Broadway, and *Einstein on the Beach*, at the Metropolitan Opera House. In addition to being seen in the United States, these works and others with Wilson have been presented on tour in France, Italy, Holland, Switzerland, Germany, Denmark, Belgium, Yugoslavia, Brazil and Iran. Wilson's own dances have been seen at the Brooklyn Academy of Music, the Museum of Modern Art, Pace University, the Merce Cunningham Studio and the Dance Umbrella, all in New York.

Abroad, deGroat has shown his works at the Autumn Festival and the International Festival of Dance in Paris and the Festival of Arts in Shiraz, Iran. He has participated in teaching and performing residencies at Cornell University, Ithaca, New York; the Walker Art Center, Minneapolis; the Nova Scotia College of Art and Design, Halifax, and the Mo Ming Collection, Chicago. DeGroat has used music by composers Philip Glass, Alan Lloyd and Michael Galasso. An extraordinary element of deGroat's works has been the use of text as an accompaniment and typewritten designs for sets and posters.

DeGroat's works are often soothing by virtue of their repetitiveness and humor. In *Angie's Waltz* he has one dancer, dressed in an oversized down parka, zigzag through the other dancers, who are waltzing calmly. They also can be breathtaking, as in *Rope Dance Translations,* when he has each dancer performing in a pool of light in an almost trancelike concentration, maneuvering ropes around their bodies with grace and beauty.

Right: Rather than employing illustrations or photographs in his graphic pieces, deGroat makes inventive use of type and lettering on the poster illustrated here.

Left: A black-and-white piece that is simple and direct. All pertinent information is typed neatly across the page and blown up for easy reading. Designed by Andrew deGroat and Christopher Knowles.

"angie's waltz"
and other dances by andy degroat
to ballet music by alan lloyd with
eighteen dancers and musicians
reservations necessary 226·8971
cunningham studio westbeth
tickets $3.50 or tdf + $1
saturday and sunday
october 15th and 16th
ritty ann burchfield
garry reigenborn
frank conversano
gail donnenfeld
michael galasso
jeff friedman
carol mullins
sheryl sutton
laura epstein
cameron burke
jessica fogel
gene rickard
meg eginton
arnie zane
randi fair
kit cation
deni bank
7:30 and 9pm

Met "Summerdance" Series

Banners, flags and posters dominated the front of the United States' largest opera house — the Metropolitan — located in New York City's Lincoln Center, announcing the 1978 "Summerdance" series. Four companies from all over the world appeared in "Summerdance," which ran almost continuously from June 13 to July 29, when the Metropolitan would otherwise have stood empty and dark. The Ballet Nacional de Cuba inaugurated the series; the Martha Graham Dance Company followed; after that came The Performing Arts Company of the People's Republic of China; and the series concluded with the London Festival Ballet. Each of the four large posters which were hung in glass cases in front of the opera house suggested the personality of the company and its repertory: the Ballet Nacional de Cuba, fiery; the Martha Graham Dance Company, historic; The Performing Arts Company of the People's Republic of China, exotic; and the London Festival Ballet, dramatic.

The tour of the United States by The Performing Arts Company of the People's Republic of China marked the first time the American public has had the opportunity to view a cross section of Chinese theater, dance and music, both old and new. Programs included acrobatics, classical and modern instrumental music, vocal music, elaborately and authentically costumed Chinese ethnic dances and modern Chinese ballet. This tour, which took over two years to arrange, was preceded in 1972 by the Shenyeng Acrobatic Troupe. Brought to the United States by the National Committee on United States–China Relations, it initiated the U.S. performing-arts exchange with the People's Republic of China.

The London Festival Ballet staged Nureyev's *Romeo and Juliet* as part of the "Summerdance" series, choreographed by and starring Nureyev. This English company, which grew out of a touring company headed by Alicia Markova and Anton Dolin in 1949, is now directed by one of its outstanding former dancers, Beryl Grey. In 1950, as Festival Ballet, it presented its first London season and featured numerous guest stars, including Leonide Massine, David Lichine and Tatiana Riaboushinska.

From its base at the Royal Festival Hall in London, the company travels extensively. It was the first English company to dance in Monte Carlo (1951) and has visited Canada, the United States, South America and the Near East. In keeping with its reputation for presenting outstanding guest artists, the Ballet was joined for its Met run by Rudolf Nureyev. Other guest artists have included Alexandra Danilova, Tamara Toumanova and Beryl Grey. In its ranks the company has featured such prominent dancers as Violette Verdy, Jeanette Monty and Oleg Briansky. Though Markova left in 1952, Dolin remained as artistic director until he was succeeded in 1961 by John Gilpin, who was also a leading male dancer with the London Festival Ballet. He in turn was followed in 1965 by Norman McDowell, who had previously been working with his own small experimental group. The London Festival Ballet's repertory is composed of the standard classics, many Michel Fokine ballets, works of the Royal Danish Ballet and many contemporary choreographers.

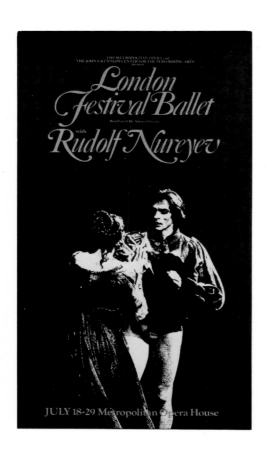

Right: A classic-style gold, red and white poster that captures the humor and cunning of the popular Peking Opera character the Monkey King. Holding a white peach in each hand, he seems to be caught in the midst of one of his mischievous antics. Based on a well-known Chinese myth, *Monkey Makes Havoc in Heaven* proved to be one of the favorite offerings of The Performing Arts Company of the People's Republic of China during its visit to the Metropolitan Opera House.

Left: A stark and foreboding black-and-white poster freezes the doomed lovers in a furtive moment of meeting — or parting — in Rudolf Nureyev's *Romeo and Juliet*.